Starting a Business Toolkit

Small Business Startup Toolbox, Featuring How to
Start a Business Manual, Business Plan Workbook,
Starting Small Business Software, Starting Your
Own Business Video Guides

MEIR LIRAZ

Published by BizMove
www.bizmove.com

ISBN- 9781794301375

Table of Contents

You may want to download the MS Word version of the planner, allowing you to work on it on your computer or print it out (see item B in the appendix)

Appendix: 49
Starting a Business Set of Tools (download instructions are provided in the appendix at the end of the book):

A. How to Start a Small Business Manual (PDF eBook)

B. Starting a Small Business Planner (MS Word)

C. Business Plan Template (MS Word)

D. Starting a Business Software

E. How to Write a Business Plan (Video Guide)

F. How to Be a Great Manager and Leader (Video Guide)

G. How to Better Manage Yourself for Success (Video Guide)

H. Start-Up Costs Worksheet (Excel)

I. The Entrepreneur Quiz

1. Preliminary Analysis

This guide is a small business startup planner, the questions concentrate on areas you must consider seriously to determine if your idea represents a real business opportunity and if you can really know what you are getting into. Use it to evaluate your new venture idea.

Perhaps the most crucial problem you will face after expressing an interest in starting a new business will be determining the feasibility of your idea. Getting into the right business at the right time is simple advice, but advice that is extremely difficult to implement. The high failure rate of new businesses and products indicates that not every idea results in successful business ventures, even when introduced by well established firm. Too many entrepreneurs strike out on a business venture so convinced of its merits that they fail to thoroughly evaluate its potential.

This planner should be useful to you in evaluating a business idea. It is designed to help you screen out ideas that are likely to fail before you invest extensive time, money, and effort in them.

Preliminary Analysis

This planner involves gathering, analyzing and evaluating information with the purpose of answering the question: "Should I go into this business?" Answering this question involves first a preliminary assessment of both personal and project considerations.

General Personal Considerations

The first seven questions ask you to do a little introspection. Are your personality characteristics such that you can both adapt to and enjoy business ownership/management?

1. Do you like to make your own decisions?

2. Do you enjoy competition?

3. Do you have will power and self-discipline?

4. Do you plan ahead?

5. Do you get things done on time?

6. Can you take advice from others?

7. Are you adaptable to changing conditions?

The next series of questions stress the physical, emotional, and financial strains of a new business.

8. Do you understand that owning your own business may entail working 12 to 16 hours a day, probably six days a week, and maybe on holidays?

9. Do you have the physical stamina to handle a business?

10. Do you have the emotional strength to withstand the strain?

11. Are you prepared to lower your standard of living for several months or years?

12. Are you prepared to lose your savings?

Specific Personal Considerations

1. Do you know which skills and areas of expertise are critical to the success of your project?

2. Do you have these skills?

3. Does your idea effectively utilize your own skills and abilities?

4. Can you find personnel that have the expertise you lack?

5. Do you know why you are considering this project?

6. Will your project effectively meet your career aspirations?

The next three questions emphasize the point that very few people can claim expertise in all phases of a feasibility study. You should realize your personal limitations and seek appropriate assistance where necessary (i.e. marketing, legal, and financial).

7. Do you have the ability to perform this feasibility study?

8. Do you have the time to perform the feasibility study?

9. Do you have the money to pay for the feasibility study done?

General Project Description

1. Briefly describe the business you want to enter.

2. List the products and/or services you want to sell

3. Describe who will use your products/services

4. Why would someone buy your product/service?

5. What kind of location do you need in terms of type of neighborhood, traffic count, nearby firms, etc.?

6. List your product/services suppliers.

7. List your major competitors - those who sell or provide like products/services.

8. List the labor and staff you require to provide your products/services.

2. Requirements for Success

To determine whether your idea meets the basic requirements for a successful new project, you must be able to answer at least one of the following questions with a "yes."

1. Does the product/service/business serve a presently unserved need?

2. Does the product/service/business serve an existing market in which demand exceeds supply?

3. Can the product/service/business successfully compete with an existing competition because of an "advantageous situation," such as better price, location, quality, etc.?

Major Flaws

A "Yes" response to questions such as the following would indicate that the idea has little chance for success.

1. Are there any causes (i.e., restrictions, monopolies, shortages) that make any of the required factors of production unavailable (i.e., unreasonable cost, scarce skills, energy, material, equipment, processes, technology, or personnel)?

2. Are capital requirements for entry or continuing operations excessive?

3. Is adequate financing hard to obtain?

4. Are there potential detrimental environmental effects?

5. Are there factors that prevent effective marketing?

3. Desired Income

Besides return on investment, you need to know the income and expenses for your business. You show profit or loss and derive operating ratios on the income statement. Dollars are the (actual, estimated, or industry average) amounts for income and expense categories. Operating ratios are expressed as percentages of net sales and show relationships of expenses and net sales.

For instance 50,000 in net sales equals 100% of sales income (revenue). Net profit after taxes equals 3.14% of net sales. The hypothetical "X" industry average after tax net profit might be 5% in a given year for firms with 50,000 in net sales. First you estimate or forecast income (revenue) and expense dollars and ratios for your business. Then compare your estimated or actual performance with your industry average. Analyze differences to see why you are doing better or worse than the competition or why your venture does or doesn't look like it will float.

These basic financial statistics are generally available for most businesses from trade and industry associations, government agencies, universities and private companies and banks

Forecast your own income statement. Do not be influenced by industry figures. Your estimates must be as accurate as possible or else you will have a false impression.

1. What is the normal markup in this line of business. i.e., the dollar difference between the cost of goods sold and sales, expressed as a percentage of sales?

2. What is the average cost of goods sold percentage of sales?

3. What is the average inventory turnover, i.e., the number of times the average inventory is sold each year?

4. What is the average gross profit as a percentage of sales?

5. What are the average expenses as a percentage of sales?

6. What is the average net profit as a percent of sales?

The following questions should remind you that you must seek both a return on your investment in your own business as well as a reasonable salary for the time you spend in operating that business.

1. How much income do you desire?

2. Are you prepared to earn less income in the first 1-3 years?

3. What minimum income do you require?

4. What financial investment will be required for your business?

5. How much could you earn by investing this money?

6. How much could you earn by working for someone else?

7. Add the amounts in 5 and 6. If this income is greater than what you can realistically expect from your business, are you prepared to forego this additional income just to be your own boss with the only prospects of more substantial profit/income in future years?

8. What is the average return on investment for a business of your type?

Expenses

1. Do you know what your expenses will be for: rent, wages, insurance, utilities, advertising, interest, etc?

2. Do you need to know which expenses are Direct, Indirect, or Fixed?

3. Do you know how much your overhead will be?

4. Do you know how much your selling expenses will be?

2. Can you minimize any of these major risks?

3. Are there major risks beyond your control?

4. Can these risks bankrupt you? (fatal flaws)

How Much Money Is Needed

Side note: You may want to use the 'Starting a Business Software' for the financial projections in this part (see item D in the appendix)

Money is a tool you can use to make your plan work. Money is also a measuring device. You will measure your plan in terms of dollars; and outsiders, such as bankers and other lenders, will do the same.

When you determine how much money is needed to start your business, you can decide whether or not to move ahead. If the cost is greater than the profits which the business can make, there are two things to consider. Many businesses do not show a profit until the second or third year of operation. If this looks like the case with your business, you will need the plans and financial reserves to carry you through this period. On the other hand, maybe you would be better off putting your money into stocks, bonds or other reliable investments rather than taking on the time consuming job of managing a business.

Miscellaneous

1. Are you aware of the major risks associated with your product? Service Business?

Like most businesses, your new business may require a loan. The burden of proof in borrowing money is upon the borrower. You have to show the banker or other lender how the borrowed money will be spent. Even more important, the lender needs to know how and when you will repay the loan.

To determine whether or not your plan is economically feasible, you need to pull together three sets of figures:

(1) Expected sales and expense figures for 12 months.

(2) Cash flow figures for 12 months.

(3) Current balance sheet figures.

Than visit your banker. Remember, your banker or lender is your friend not your enemy. So, meet regularly. Share all the information and data you possess. If the lender is ready to help, he (or she) needs to know not only your strengths but also your weaknesses.

Expected Sales and Expenses Figures

To determine whether or not your business can make its way in the market place, you should estimate your sales and expenses for 12 months. The form which follows is designed to help you in this task.

Projected Statement of Sales and Expenses for One Year

	Jan	Feb	Mar	Apr	Etc.	Total
A. Net Sales	—	—	—	—	—	—
B. Cost of Goods Sold	—	—	—	—	—	—
1. Raw Materials	—	—	—	—	—	—
2. Direct Labor	—	—	—	—	—	—
3. Manufacturing Overhead	—	—	—	—	—	—
Indirect Labor	—	—	—	—	—	—
Factory Heat & Power	—	—	—	—	—	—
Insurance and Taxes	—	—	—	—	—	—
Depreciation	—	—	—	—	—	—
C. Gross Margin (Subtract B from A)	—	—	—	—	—	—
D. Selling and Administrative Expenses	—	—	—	—	—	—
4. Salaries and Commissions	—	—	—	—	—	—
5. Advertising Expenses	—	—	—	—	—	—
6. Miscellaneous Expenses	—	—	—	—	—	—
E. Net Operating Profit (Subtract D from C)	—	—	—	—	—	—
F. Interest Expense	—	—	—	—	—	—
G. Net Profit before Taxes (Subtract F from E)	—	—	—	—	—	—
H. Estimated Income Tax	—	—	—	—	—	—
I. Net Profit after Income Tax (Subtract H from G)	—	—	—	—	—	—

Cash Flow Figures

Estimates of future sales will not pay an owner-manager's bills. Cash must flow into the business at the proper times if bills are to be paid and a profit realized at the end of the year. To determine whether your projected sales and expense figures are realistic, you should prepare a cash flow forecast for the 12 months covered by your estimates of sales and expenses.

The form that follow were designed to help you estimate your cash situation and to get the appropriate figures on paper.

Estimated Cash Forecast

Jan Feb Mar Apr Etc.

(1) Cash in Bank
(Start of Month) ___ ___ ___ ___ ___
(Start of Month) ___ ___ ___ ___ ___

(3) Total Cash
(add (1) and (2) ___ ___ ___ ___ ___

(4) Expected Accounts
Receivable ___ ___ ___ ___ ___

(5) Other Money
Expected ___ ___ ___ ___ ___

(6) Total Receipts

(add (4) and (5)) ___ ___ ___ ___ ___

Receipts (add (3)
and (6) ___ ___ ___ ___ ___

(8) All Disbursements
(for month) ___ ___ ___ ___ ___

(9) Cash Balance at end of Month
in Bank Account and Petty Cash

(subtract (8) from (7)* ___ ___ ___ ___ ___
*This balance is your starting figure for the
next month

Current Balance Sheet Figures

A balance sheet shows the financial conditions of a business as of a certain date. It lists what a business has, what it owes, and the investment of the owner. A balance sheet enable you to see at a glance your assets and liabilities.

Use the blanks below to draw up a current balance sheet for your company.

Current Balance Sheet
for: (Name of your company)
As of: (Date)

Assets	**Liabilities**
Current Assets	**Current Liabilities**
Cash_____	Accounts payable_____
Accounts Receivable_____	
Accrued Expenses_____	
Inventory_____	Short Term Loans_____
Fixed Assets	**Fixed Liabilities**
Land_____	Long Term Loan_____
Building_____	Mortgage_____
Equipment_____	
Total_____	Net worth_____
Less depreciation_____	_____
Total_____	**Total**_____

4. Marketing

Successful marketing starts with you, the owner-manager. You have to know your product, your market, your customers, and your competition.

You have to decide who your market is, where it is, why they will buy your product, whether it is a growth or static market, if there are any seasonal aspects of the market, and what percentage of the market you will shoot for in the first, second, and third year of operation. Your goals and plans must be based on and be responsive to this kind of fact finding.

The narrative and work blocks that follow are designed to help you work out a marketing plan. Your objective is to determine what needs to be done to bring in sales dollars.

Market Area

Where and to whom are you going to sell your product? Describe the market area you will serve in terms of geography and customer profile:

Distribution

How will you get your product to the ultimate consumer? Will you sell it directly through your own sales organization or indirectly through agents, brokers, wholesalers, and so on. (Use the blank to write a brief statement of your method of distribution and manner of sales):

What will this method of distribution cost you?

Do you plan to use special marketing, sales or merchandising techniques? Describe them here:

Market Trends

What has been the sales trend in your market area for your principal product(s) over the last 5 years? What do you expect it to be 5 years from now? You should indicate the source of your data and the basis of your projections. (This is a marketing research problem. It will require you to do some digging in order to come up with a market projection. Trade Associations will probably be your most helpful source of information. The Bureau of Census publishes a great deal of useful statistics). Industry and product statistics are usually indicated in dollars, Units, such as numbers of customers, numbers of items sold, etc., may be used, but also relate your sales to dollars.

List the names and addresses of trade associations which serve your industry and indicate whether or not you are a member.

List the names and addresses of other organizations, governmental agencies, industry and indicate whether or not you are a member.

Share of the Market

What percentage of total sales in your market area do you expect to obtain for your products after your facility is in full operation?

Products or Products Category	Local Market (%)	Total Market (%)
_____	_____	_____
_____	_____	_____

Sales Volume

What sales volume do you expect to reach with your products?

	Total Sales	Product(s)1	Product(s)2
First Year	$_____	$_____	$_____
Units	_____	_____	_____
Second Year	$_____	$_____	$_____
Units	_____	_____	_____
Third Year	$_____	$_____	$_____
Units	_____	_____	_____

5. Competition

Who Are Your Competitors?

List your principal competitors selling in your market area estimate their percentage of market penetration and dollar sales in that market, and estimate their potential loss of sales as a result of your entry into the market.

Name of Competitor and Location	% Share of Market	Estimated Sales	Sales Loss Because of You
1. _____	_____	_____	_____
2. _____	_____	_____	_____
3. _____	_____	_____	_____
4. _____	_____	_____	_____

How Do You Rate Your Competition?

Try to find out the strengths and weaknesses of each competitor. Then write your opinion of each of your principal competitors, their principal products, facilities, marketing characteristics, and new product development or adaptability to changing market conditions.

Have any of your competitors recently closed operations or have they withdrawn from your market area? (State reasons if you know them):

Advantages Over Competitors

On what basis will you be able to capture your projected share of the market? Below is a list of characteristics which may indicate the advantages your product(s) enjoy over those offered by competitors. Indicate those advantages by placing a check in the proper space. If there is more than one competitor, you may want to make more than one checklist. Attach these to the worksheet.

Analyze each characteristic. For example, a higher price may not be a disadvantage if the product is of higher quality than your competitor's. You may want to make a wish to spell out the specifics of each characteristic and explain where your product is disadvantaged and how this will be overcome,

42

attach it to this worksheet. Also, the unique characteristics of your product can be the basis for advertising and sales promotion.

Remember, the more extensive your planning, the more your business plan will help you.

Product(s)	Product No. 1	Product No. 2
Price		
Performance		
Durability		
Versatility		
Speed or accuracy		
Ease of operation or use		
Ease of maintenance or repair		
Ease or cost of installation		
Size or weight		
Styling or appearance		
Other characteristics not listed:		

_____

_____

What, if anything, is unique about your product?

6. Sales

1. Determine the total sales volume in your market area.

2. How accurate do you think your forecast of total sales is?

3. Did you base your forecast on concrete data?

4. Is the estimated sales figure "normal" for your market area?

5. Is the sales per square foot for your competitors above the normal average?

6. Are there conditions, or trends, that could change your forecast of total sales?

7. Do you expect to carry items in inventory from season to season, or do you plan to mark down products occasionally to eliminate inventories? If you do not carry over inventory, have you adequately considered the effect of mark-down in your pricing? (Your gross profits margin may be too low.)

8. How do you plan to advertise and promote your product/service/business?

9. Forecast the share of the total market that you can realistically expect - as a dollar amount and as a percentage of your market.

10. Are you sure that you can create enough competitive advantages to achieve the market share in your forecast of the previous question?

11. Is your forecast of dollar sales greater than the sales amount needed to guarantee your desired or minimum income?

12. Have you been optimistic or pessimistic in your forecast of sales?

13. Do you need to hire an expert to refine the sales forecast?

14. Are you willing to hire an expert to refine the sales forecast?

7. Supply

1. Can you make a list of every item of inventory and operating supplies needed?

2. Do you know the quantity, quality, technical specifications, and price ranges desired?

3. Do you know the name and location of each potential source of supply?

4. Do you know the price ranges available for each product from each supplier?

5. Do you know about the delivery schedules for each supplier?

6. Do you know the sales terms of each supplier?

7. Do you know the credit terms of each supplier?

8. Do you know the financial condition of each supplier?

9. Is there a risk of shortage for any critical materials or merchandise?

10. Are you aware of which supplies have an advantage relative to transportation costs?

11. Will the price available allow you to achieve an adequate markup?

8. Getting the work Done

Your business is only part way home when you have planned your marketing. Organization is needed if your business is to produce what you expect it to produce.

Organization is essential because you as the owner-manager probably cannot do all the work.

You'll have to delegate work, responsibility, and authority. A helpful tool in getting this done is the organization chart. It shows at a glance who is responsible for the major activities of a business. However, no matter how your operation is organized, keep control of the financial management.

In the beginning, the owner of the small business probably does everything.

It is important that you recognize your weaknesses early in the game and plan to get assistance wherever you need it. This may be done using consultants on an as-needed basis, by hiring the needed personnel, or by retaining a lawyer and accountant.

The work blocks below lists some of the areas you may want to consider. Adapt it to your needs and indicate who will take care of the various functions. (One name may appear more than once.)

Manufacturing

Marketing

Research and Technical Backup

Accounting

Legal

Insurance

Other:

9. Making Your Plan Work

To make your plan work you will need feedback. For example, the yearend profit and loss (income) statement shows whether your business made a profit or loss for the past 12 months.

But you can't wait 12 months for the score. To keep your plan on target you need readings at frequent intervals. A profit and loss statement at the end of each month or at the end of each quarter is one type of frequent feedback. However, the P and L may be more of a loss than a profit statement if you rely only on it. In addition, your cash flow projection must be continuously updated and revised as necessary. You must set up management controls which will help you insure that the right things are being done from day to day and from week to week.

The management control system which you set up should give you precise information on: inventory, production, quality, sales, collection of accounts receivable, and disbursement. The simpler the system, the better. Its purpose is to give you and your key people current information in time to correct deviations from approved policies, procedures, or practices. You are after facts with emphasis on trouble spots.

Inventory Control

The purpose of controlling inventory is to provide maximum service to your customers. Your aim should be to achieve a rapid turnover on your inventory, the fewer dollars you tie up in raw materials inventory and in finished goods inventory, the better. Or, saying it in reverse, the faster you get back your investment in raw materials and finished goods inventory, the faster you can reinvest your capital to meet additional consumer needs.

In setting up inventory controls, keep in mind that the cost of the inventory is not your only cost. There are inventory costs, such as the cost of purchasing, the cost of keeping inventory records, and the cost of receiving and storing raw materials.

Production

In preparing this business planner, you have estimated the cost figures for your operations. Use these figures as the basis for standards against which you can measure your day-to-day operations to make sure that the clock does not nibble away at profits. These standards will help you to keep machine time, labor man-hours, process time, delay time, and down time within your projected cost figures. Periodic reports will allow you to keep your finger on potential drains on your profits and should also provide feedback on your overhead expense.

Quality Control

Poorly made products cause a company to lose customers. In addition, when a product fails to perform satisfactorily, shipments are held up, inventory is increased, and a severe financial strain can result. Moreover, when quality is poor, it's a good bet that waste and spoilage are greater than they should be. The details - checkpoints, reports and so on - of your quality control system will depend on your type of production system. In working out these details, keep in mind that their purpose is to answer one question: What needs to be done to see that the work is right the first time? Will you have to do extensive quality control on raw materials? This is an added expense you must consider.

Sales

To keep on top of sales, you will need answers to questions, such as: How many sales were made? What was the dollar amount? What products were sold? At what price? What delivery dates were promised? What credit terms were given to customers?

It is also important that you set up an effective collection system for "accounts receivable," so that you don't tie up your capital in aging accounts.

Disbursement

Your management controls should also give you information about the dollars your company pays out. In checking on your bills, you do not want to be penny-wise and pound-foolish. You need to know that major items, such as paying bills on time get the supplier's discount, are being handled according to your policies. Your review system should also give you the opportunity to make judgments on the use of funds. In this manner, you can be on top of emergencies as well as routine situations. Your system should also keep you aware that tax moneys, such as payroll income tax deductions, are set aside and paid out at the proper time.

Break-Even

Break-even analysis is a management control device because the break-even point shows about how much you must sell under given conditions in order to just cover your costs with No profit and No loss.

In preparing to start a business you should determine at what approximate level of sales a new product will pay for itself and begin to bring in a profit.

Profit depends on sales volume, selling price, and costs. So, to figure your break-even point, first separate your fixed costs, such as rent or depreciation allowance, from your variable costs per unit, such as direct labor and materials.

The formula is:

$$\text{Break-even volume} = \frac{\text{Total fixed costs}}{\text{Selling price - variable cost per unit}}$$

For example, Gore Plastics has determined its fixed costs to be $100,000 and variable costs to be $50 per unit. If the selling price per unit is $100, then Ajax's break-even volume is

$$\text{Break-even volume} = \frac{\$100,000}{\$100 - \$50} = 2000 \text{ units}$$

Earlier you estimated your expected sales for each product and total sales. Compute the break-even point for each.

Product 1: _____   Product 2: _____

Total Sales: _____

10. Venture Feasibility

1. Are there any major questions remaining about your proposed venture?

2. Do the above questions arise because of a lack of data?

3. Do the above questions arise because of a lack of management skills?

4. Do the above questions arise because of a "fatal flaw" in your idea?

5. Can you obtain the additional data needed?

11. Keeping Your Plan Up-To-Date

The best made business planner gets out of date because conditions change. Sometimes the change is with customers. Their desires and tastes shift. For example, a new idea can sweep the county in 6 months and die overnight. Sometimes the change is technological as when new raw materials and components are put on the market.

In order to adjust a business planner to account for such changes, an you must:

(1) Be alert to the changes that come about in your industry, in your market, and in your community.

(2) Check your plan against these changes.

(3) Determine what revisions, if any, are needed in your plan.

When judgments are wrong, cut your losses as soon as possible and learn from the experience. The mental anguish caused by wrong judgments is part of the price you pay for being your own boss. You get your rewards from the satisfaction and profits that result from correct judgments.

Keep in mind that few business owners are right 100 percent of the time. They can improve their batting average by operating with a business plan and by keeping that plan up to date.

That concludes the Starting a Business Planner...

12. Bonus Chapter (1): Frequently Asked Questions about Starting a Business

To start and run a small business you must know and be many things. As one small business owner attending a conference put it: "When I came here, my business lost the services of its chief executive, sales manager, controller, advertising department, personnel director, head bookkeeper, and janitor."

This chapter, based on questions asked by people in small business or contemplating starting, suggests the many facets of running a small concern that each owner/manager must become familiar with.

While the answers to the questions are hardly exhaustive of any of the subjects, they provide the background for questions you may need to ask before going into business, as well as suggesting sources of answers to those questions.

Starting Business Advice

Almost everyone considering it has dozens of questions about starting a small business. The only foolish questions, of course, are the questions that aren't asked. Yet, many times we don't have enough information to ask the right questions.

The questions in this chapter are drawn from participants in training courses for new entrepreneurs. Most of the questioners didn't own, operate, or manage small businesses. Their questions are typical of what's on the minds of potential business owners. You may have pondered similar questions, as you thought about becoming your own boss.

The questions fell generally into areas such as the steps in setting up a business, marketing, and financing a new concern. In this chapter the questions have been grouped by subject.

Answers to the questions came from experts in the various areas. These experts include a lawyer, an accountant, a bank loan officer, several small business owners, and market researchers.

These answers, it is hoped, will help you as you approach deciding on becoming a small business owner.

The questions may suggest questions that you should find answers to before you invest your money, time, and effort in a small business.

Starting Out

1. If you have money but no particular business in mind, how can you get enough

information on the best business to go into?

The best way of choosing your business venture is to look at your experience and educational background. A thorough review will provide leads on the business field you should enter - do what you know best. Even more important, you must like the business field you are going to enter to bring the enthusiasm and self-confidence you need to make the business go.

2. What are the basic survival skills you need to run a business?

The basic survival skills include a working knowledge of basic record keeping; financial management; personnel management; market analysis; break-even analysis; product or service knowledge; tax knowledge; legal structures; and communication skills.

3. What special obstacles do women entering business face, and how can these obstacles be overcome?

Women are at last making inroads into business, not only as executives but as owners. There are many obstacles, chief among them the doubts that lenders, suppliers, and in some fields, customers have about women's ability to run businesses. These can be overcome with self confidence and a strong belief in your ideas. You should not be discouraged by being rebuffed by people who simply don't understand. As more and more women enter business and succeed, the process will become easier and easier.

4. What are the most important factors that cause small business failure?

There are, of course, many reasons for the failure of new small businesses. One way of looking at the causes is to remember that a new business is starting at zero momentum; newly entering a market, having to establish supplier relations, finding proper financing, and training employees. To coordinate all these facets and start them simultaneously is a tremendous job. If you don't have experience and management capability, success won't be very likely. You'll also find that under-capitalized businesses, those without enough cash to carry them through the first six months or so before the business starts making money, don't have good survival prospects. In such cases, even businesses with good management can founder.

5. If you're trying to buy a going service business, how can you figure a reasonable price for the business that takes into account goodwill and business contacts in addition to the value of equipment and inventory?

There are many methods, but basically what you're trying to do is set a value on the assets and earnings record of the firm. The simplest way is to determine the "payback period," usually two or three years. That is, the net profit for two years would equal the goodwill value. A more complicated and accurate method called the "net present value" method, is based on the cost of capital and a risk factor. For that method an accountant's help would be valuable.

6. What kind of a market study should you do before deciding to buy a radio station?

Determining the price of any business is difficult. For a radio station specifically, you can get the figures on the total revenue of all stations in the area (that is, advertising revenue). You should also get the percentage of the total market that the station you're considering has. You must also determine the potential market for the area in advertising dollars. Finding out the total number of businesses by line and size in the area covered by the station and their advertising expenditures would give you some insight. Really, you'd study the market like this for buying any business.

7. How long does it take a new business to establish a good public image?

A good public image takes a long time to

establish (and only minutes to lose). There is no set formula, but a good image depends on:

- The service, products, and customer treatment you provide;
- The market you're in;
- How you stack up against your competitors;
- The quality of your public relations and advertising programs.

If you're new to a market - and if you do what you say you're going to - you may establish an excellent reputation in 18 to 24 months.

8. How do you find a good lawyer?

As with most personal services, you must have rapport with your attorney. The best way to determine this is to talk to lawyers by phone or visit them before you make a selection. Get recommendations from friends, or your banker. You're looking for someone you can trust and who will take an interest in you and your business.

9. Do you need a lawyer to start a business?

No, but it's wise to get the best advice possible when you're starting out. An attorney is one source of the expertise you'll need to draw on.

Setting Up Business Form of Business

10. What form of business do you recommend for a new business?

Each legal form, sole proprietorship, partnership, or corporation, has its advantages and disadvantages. The one you should pick depends on your circumstances, including:

- Your financial condition,
- The line of business you're entering,
- The number of employees,
- The risk involved,
- Your tax situation.

Don't assume, if you plan a one-person business, that sole proprietorship is the way to go. See your lawyer.

The Market

11. How can you find out what the prevailing costs are for a service business in your market area?

One way is simply to call competitors and ask their prices. Their prices will give you a lead. You could ask competitors' customers for the same information if you didn't want to go directly to the competition.

12. How do you go about determining the market for a mail order business?

The principles of determining market share and market potential are the same no matter how large the geographical area. You must first determine a customer profile, the size of the market, and the number of competitors. You could also use a readership survey given to you by a magazine in which you intend to advertise.

Pricing

13. How do you figure markup and markdown?

Markup (markon) is the original amount that the merchandise is marked up. Markup as a percentage (also called gross margin rate) is figured as a percentage of sales. For example, say the cost of merchandise is $10 and you want a 20 percent markup; what is the selling price (SP)? By definition we know that markup as a percentage is given as a percentage of sales. Thus, our cost must be 80 percent of the selling price (100 percent selling price - 20 percent desired markup).

So, our selling price is $12.50, cost $10.00, and markup $2.50 or 20 percent of the selling price.

Markdown (discount) is a reduction of selling price below the original sale price. Assume the item is marked down to $11.25. The markdown is $1.25 or a 10 percent markdown ($1.25 markdown divided by $12.50 original selling price).

14. How would you go about establishing price guidelines for a business renting items to customers?

Pricing is based normally on a combination of cost and market competition. Trade associations are a prime source of such information.

Finances

15. What is the average expected net profit for small business?

Average net profits vary with the type of business - retail, wholesale, service, manufacturing, construction. They also vary for the type of business structure - proprietorship or corporation. Dun & Bradstreet publish ratios which give you these figures, as well as lots of very useful cost information.

16. Would you explain the meaning of "rate of return on investment"? How is it different from net profit? Is it different from return on assets employed?

Net profit (before taxes) is basically total sales for a specific period less cost of goods and operating expenses during that period. (For a retail business, cost of goods would be your cost of merchandise sold.) Net profit is a function of both rate of return on investment (ROI) and return on total assets. ROI is net profit divided by capital invested by the owners of the company.

ROI is used to measure the effectiveness of management in attaining the owners' desired return on their investment. Generally, the larger the ROI, the more attractive a company is to potential investors.

Return on total assets is the net profit divided by total assets. This measures the net profitability of the use of all resources of the business. It is another tool for measuring management effectiveness in the use of all resources borrowed and equity.

17. Does a bank require absolute top credit references from loan applicants?

The better the credit references the greater the possibility of loan approval.

18. If I estimate my start-up cost at $50,000 and can't put up anywhere near the $25,000 that I've been told is what I should have for my share, am I wasting my time even filling out a loan application?

In all probability you would be, although there are some exceptions. For example, it might be possible to get a loan under your circumstances if you were buying a business that's already operating well enough to provide sufficient profits to cover its obligations and the loan. Furthermore, if the applicant is the present manager who has made this business go, the chances of getting such a loan are much better.

Help!

19. Getting money is difficult; keeping it may be even more difficult. Where can I get assistance in managing my business?

Your accountant and bank can provide financial counseling which can be very helpful in starting and managing your business. They can also give you valuable information on the local area and your market that can be critical in making decisions in your business.

13. Bonus Chapter (2): How to Make Money with Your New Business Idea

Getting new Ideas are essential to business progress. It is very difficult, however, for innovators to get the kind of financial and management support they need to realize their ideas.

This chapter, aimed at idea people, inventors, and innovative owner-managers of businesses, describes the tests every idea must pass before it makes money.

You've Got a New Idea? Great!

So, you've had a new business idea for an invention or an innovative way of doing something that will boost productivity, put more people to work, and make lots of money for you and anyone who back you? As you've probably heard, you're the kind of person your country needs to compete in world markets and maintain its standard of living. You're the cutting edge of the future.

You are another of those individuals on whom progress has always depended. We all know that it hasn't been huge corporations that have come up with the inventions that have revolutionized life. As the discoverer of penicillin, Sir Alexander Flemming, said, "It is the lone worker who makes the first advance in a subject: The details may be worked out by a team, but the prime idea is due to the enterprise, thought and perception of an individual." Innovators like you are business's lifeblood.

Owner-managers who have started businesses on new ideas know first hand about the innovation process. They also know that you can expect to hear...

You've Got a New Business Idea? So What?

In the first place, the chances that you are the first to come up with a particular innovation are somewhere between slim and none. Secondly, even if you have come up with the better mouse trap, nobody - but nobody - is going to beat a path to your door. In fact, in the course of trying to peddle your BMT, you'll beat up plenty of shoe leather wearing paths to other people's doors. You'll stand a good chance of wearing out your patience and several dozen crying towels as well.

Well, new product failure rates are estimated conservatively to be between 50 and 80 percent. One survey of major companies with millions of dollars to spend of R & D, market research, and product advertising, and with well-established distribution systems found that of 58 internal proposals only 12 made it past initial screening. From these 12 only one successful new product emerged.

Another group set up to help innovators has found that of every 100 ideas submitted 85 have too many faults to bother with. They can be eliminated immediately. Of the remaining 15, maybe five will ever be produced. One of those might - only might - make money.

With odds like 99 to 1 against an idea being a monetary success, is it any surprise that your idea is greeted with a chorus of yawns? People - companies, investors, what have you - are basically conservative with their money. Ideas are risky.

Does that mean you should forget about your idea? Of course not. It merely means that now you're beginning to see what Edison meant, when he said, "Genius is one percent inspiration and ninety-nine percent perspiration."

Again, those of you who own small firms started on innovations are well aware of the truth of Edison's words. You've been through the hard work.

Can You Exploit Your New Business Ideas?

Although coming up with what you think is a sure-fire idea is the biggest step, it's still only the first one. You've got the other thousand miles of the journey to success still ahead of you.

Many things remain to be done before you can expect to realize the first dollar from your invention or other innovation. You should be prepared for the unhappy discovery that the end of the line for your idea may turn up well before the point you needed to reach to make money from it.

At a bare minimum, your idea will have to pass the following tests:

- Is it original or has someone else already come up with it?
- Can someone produce and distribute it if it's an invention or other product, or use it if it's a marketing innovation, a new use for an existing product or the like?
- Will it really make money? (Will someone buy it?)

Can you protect your idea?

That seems to be a modest enough list, and it is. The problems arise from the dozens of underlying questions that must be answered before the major questions can be resolved. Here, for example, are the 33 areas that the University of Oregon's Innovation Center runs each submitted idea through to determine if it has commercial merit:

- Legality
- Safety
- Environmental Impact
- Societal Impact
- Potential Market
- Product Life Cycle
- Usage Learning
- Product Visibility
- Service
- Durability
- New Competition
- Functional Feasibility
- Production Feasibility
- Stability of Demand
- Consumer
- User Compatibility
- Marketing Research
- Distribution
- Perceived Function
- Existing Competition
- Potential Sales
- Development Status
- Investment Costs
- Trend of Demand
- Product Line Potential
- Need
- Promotion
- Appearance
- Price
- Protection
- Payback Period

- Profitability
- Product Interdependence
- Research and Development

Now that is not a modest list. However, for the moment let's ignore the 33 and look at the four broad questions.

Is Your New Business Ideas Original?

Obviously, if somebody has already come up with and produced as good an item or a better one, it would be pointless for you to pursue a similar idea any further. You'd only be wasting your time and money.

There are lots of places to look to find out. If your idea is for a consumer product, check stores and catalogs. Check trade associations and trade publication in the field into which your invention or innovation fits. Visit trade shows relevant to your idea. Look in the business and popular press.

Don't be afraid to ask people in the field if they've ever heard of anything along the lines of your idea. In the pure idea stage it's not very likely that somebody will steal your idea - all the hard work still has to be done. Besides, you can ask general sorts of questions and keep the details of your idea to yourself if you're really anxious that your idea will be pirated. Patent rights to an idea in major foreign countries will be jeopardized by uncontrolled disclosure prior to filing a patent application in the United States.

Obviously, if what you've come up with is an invention or an idea that can be put into patentable form, you'll eventually have to make a patent search. You could do that in this early stage, but it is probably a better idea to hold off until you've taken a look at your idea in the light of the next two questions?

How Will the New Idea or Invention Be Produced and Distributed?

The first thought many innovators have is to take their ideas to a big national company. Provide the dazzling idea, they think, and let the giant work out the details. After all, the national company has the money, the production capability, and the marketing know-how to make this surefire profit maker go.

Unfortunately, the big companies are almost never interested in ideas from outsiders. Whether that's because, as one innovation broker has suggested, that outside technology is "a risk, a threat," or simply because large corporations need potential sales of an item to be in the tens of millions of dollars, doesn't matter. The cold fact is that selling a big firm on your idea is in the 100 to 1 shot range.

On the other end of the scale, you may be able to produce some items yourself, working out of your home and selling online. This method can be a good way to get started, but after a while you may find yourself getting tired of having 200,000 better mouse traps stashed in your bedroom.

To be sure, if you can start (or already have) your own company, you will be better off. It's easier to sell a company than a patent, even if the company is losing money.

Many potential buyers understand a company much better than they understand the technology of an invention. Business people usually look at the profit-and-loss possibilities differently from the way an innovator does.

Many of these business people follow what one innovator has called "the 'Anyhow' theory of economics"; we have a plant anyhow. We have a sales force anyhow. We advertise anyhow. We're smarter anyhow." Such business people also know that by the time they purchase a company most of the bugs are out of the technology and customers exist.

Between the extremes of starting your own company or having big business buy you out is taking your idea to small and medium-sized businesses. Such firms would be happy to produce an item producing sales in amounts that simply don't interest large companies.

Smaller firms may lack marketing and distribution expertise, but again your major problem is even finding one that can help you realize your idea and is interested in trying.

Will Your New Business Ideas Make Money?

This is the question that worries everybody. Here is where the risk arises that makes it so difficult to interest people in backing your idea.

It's a question that's really impossible to answer with any assurance. After all, major corporations even with massive market studies hit clinkers all the time. Remember the Edsel? On the other hand, an idea so seemingly stupid that you'd think it was somebody's idea of a silly joke might make millions. Don't you wish you'd though of the pet rock?

So many factors need to be considered to answer this question. Is there a market? Where is it? Is it concentrated or dispersed? Could the size of the market change suddenly? Will competition drive you out? These questions are by no means the bottom of the iceberg. Yet, answering the money question to the satisfaction of potential backers is the key to the other questions.

Can You Protect Your Business Ideas?

Once you've come up with tentatively satisfying answers to the originality, production and distribution, and saleability questions, it's time to consider protecting your idea. After all, looks like you may have something.

If you do have a patentable item, it's time to look into trying to protect it under the patent laws. Here briefly are the steps you'll need to follow:

Get a close friend (who understands your invention) to sign his or her name on a dated diagram or written description of the invention. Or, you can file a "disclosure document" with the Patent Office. Taking one to these measures will provide evidence of the time you came up with your invention in case of a dispute with other inventors over who conceived it first. Sending yourself a registered letter describing the invention itself is useless as evidence. Get patent protection as soon as possible.

Make a patent search to see whether or not the inventory has already been patented in as good or better version. You can make a search yourself. You may find, however that the only practical way to proceed from patent search on is with the help of a patent attorney.

If the invention has not been patented, prepare a patent application and file it with the Patent and Trademark Office.

Again, you can do this yourself, following the pattern you find in similar, recent patents, though, again, a patent attorney will be helpful. If you have an attorney prepare your application, go through the exercise yourself, anyway. Compare your application with your attorney's. Make sure all of the points you regard as important are covered and that the attorney has written what you want to say. Work out differences together.

Promptly file amendments or additional patent application with the Office if you make important changes in your invention.

Having a patent won't mean you have absolute protection. In fact, one survey found that in over 70% of infringement cases brought by patent holders to protect their patents, the patent itself was held invalid.

Defending your patent can be very expensive. If you don't have a patent, however the probability of successfully protecting your invention approaches zero.

Mere ideas or suggestions can't be patented. Some of these you may be able to be put in patentable form, but for those that you can't it's pretty much do-it-yourself. Consult with a patent attorney or the Patent Office about the classes of patentable subject matter.

Say, for example, you think you have a great gimmick for selling more of Company A's products. Leaving aside the likelihood that Company A won't be interested, how do you approach Company A with your idea with any assurance they won't simply use it without paying a cent?

About the best you can do is write them a letter telling them you have a promotional (or whatever) idea and, without giving them any details, offer to send it to them. Include in your letter a statement to be signed and returned by a Company A representative promising they won't divulge your idea or make use of it without compensation (to be negotiated between them and you), if they'd like to know the details of your plan. They'll probably say thanks but no thanks or that they can't promise any such things without seeing the idea, but it's the only course open to you.

Is There Any Hope?

Each section of this chapter seems to be packed with bad news, but this wouldn't be doing you any favors by raising false hopes. The point is, you need to be more than an idea person to make money out of an invention or other innovation.

Many small businesses have been doomed from the start because of false hopes. Those of you who already operate going firms have avoided wishful thinking in other business areas. You need to avoid it where innovation is concerned, too.

What are potential idea and invention backers looking for? If you read around the subject, you'll run across many comments to the effect that:

- What we want is an entrepreneur, someone who cannot only invent a product but find capital and a way of getting the product on the market.
- It's better to have a fair new product and a great manager than the other way around.
- Management is the most important element for success of an invention.

Edison wasn't only an inventing genius. He was also a promoting genius, a publicity genius, a capital-raising genius, a genius at seeing potential markets for inventions.

Have you ever heard of Joseph Swan? A strong case could be made for saying he invented the electric light eight months before Edison. Who got the patents? Who got the bulb to the market? Edison. Who invented the electric light bulb? Edison.

Few of us are Edisons. We may have brilliant

product ideas, but we aren't usually knowledgeable, let alone brilliant, in all of the areas that need to be covered. We need help.

Where Can You Go for Help?

While you probably still have to invest considerable perspiration yourself, you can get help with some of the sweating. Even Edison had some help.

Patent Attorneys and Agents

Attorneys and agents can help you make patent searches and applications, if you can't do them yourself. The U.S. Patent Office has geographical and alphabetical listings of such people, but doesn't make recommendations or assume any responsibility for your selection from their lists. You can also find attorneys and agents by searching the internet.

Invention Promotion Firms

Also likely to be found online are firms that offer - for a fee- to take on the whole job of protecting and promoting your idea. Caution is necessary in dealing with such promoters.

Federal Trade Commission investigations found that one firm, which charged fees ranging from $1,000 to $2,000 had ten clients who made money on their inventions - that was out of a total of 35,000. Another firm with 30,000 had only three with successful inventions. If you elect to use an idea promotion firm, make sure:

- They don't collect the entire fee in advance.
- They will provide you with samples of their promotional materials and lists of companies to whom they've sent it. (Then check with those companies yourself.)
- You check the promotion firm's reputation with the local Better Business Bureau, Chamber of Commerce, a patent attorney, or a local inventors or innovators club.

Invention Brokers

Brokers work for a portion of the profits from an invention. They may help inventors raise capital and form companies to produce and market their inventions. They often provide sophisticated management advice. In general, you can expect these brokers to be interested in more complex technology with fairly large sales potential.

University Innovation/Invention/Entrepreneurial Centers

These centers, some funded by the National Science Foundation, show promise for helping inventors and innovators. The best known one, the University of Oregon's Experimental Center for the Advancement of Invention and Innovation (The Innovation Center no longer exists), for example, evaluated an idea for a very modest fee. The Center evaluated an idea on 33 criteria (listed earlier in this chapter) to help inventors weed out bad ideas so they won't waste further time and money on them.

The Center also identified trouble spots that required special attention in planning the development or commercialization of a potential new product. If an idea looked like it had merit and was commercially feasible, the Center tried to link the innovator with established companies or referred him or her to sources of funds.

Inventor's Clubs/Associations/Societies

You may have such clubs in your locality. You can share experiences with kindred spirits and get good advice, low cost evaluation, and other help.

Talking with other inventors is probably the most helpful thing you can do. Find someone who has been through the entire routine of patents, applied R & D, and stages of financing. It doesn't matter if the end result was a financial success or failure. Getting the nitty-gritty of the process is what's important.

Are You Being Unreasonable About Your Chances?

If you have read this chapter and still think you can make money with your idea, some people might think you've missed the point. If you continue to believe in your idea after looking at the odds and obstacles, you are being unreasonable.

That's exactly what you should be. You're in good company.

All progress is made by unreasonable people. George Bernard Shaw observed: Reasonable people adapt to the world around them, unreasonable people try to change it.

Appendix: Set of Tools (With Download Links):

A. How to Start a Small Business Manual (PDF eBook) - a practical guide that will walk you step by step through all the essential phases of starting your own business. The book is packed with guides, worksheets and checklists. These strategies are absolutely crucial to your business' success yet are simple and easy to apply.

Get it from here:

https://www.bizmove.com/toolkit/start-business.htm

B. Starting a Small Business Planner (MS Word) – The full content of this book provided in MS Word format, allows you to work the planner on your computer or print it out.

Get it from here:

https://www.bizmove.com/toolkit/planner.docx

C. Business Plan Template (MS Word) – a

combination business plan sample and workbook. This is a high quality, full blown business plan template, complete with detailed instructions and all related spreadsheets. Allows you to easily prepare a professional business plan right on your computer.

Get it from here:

https://www.bizmove.com/toolkit/business -plan.htm

D. Starting a Business Software – multi featured, fully operational software program. It is a management program that will help you do the following: Plan and analyze your start up expenses and sales, prepare budgets, cash flow projections and projected income statements, perform break-even point analysis, conduct 'what-if's analysis, perform financial ratios analysis, make a "go /no-go" decision.

You also get a complete easy to understand manual that will allow you to take full advantage of the program.

Get it from here:

https://www.bizmove.com/toolkit/software .htm

E. How To Write a Business Plan (Video Guide) – an interactive video guide that will walk you step by step through all the essential phases of creating a successful business plan. It explains the importance of business planning defines and describes the business plan outline and its components, thus enabling you to develop a very good business plan.

Watch it here:

https://www.bizmove.com/toolkit/bp-video.htm

F. How to Be a Great Manager and Leader (Video Guide) - Learn how to improve your leadership skills and become a better manager and leader. Discover how to be the boss people want to give 200 percent for. In this video you'll discover 120 powerful tips and strategies to motivate and inspire your people to bring out the best in them.

Watch it here:

https://www.bizmove.com/toolkit/leader.htm

G. How to Better Manage Yourself for Success (Video Guide) - You are responsible for everything that happens in your life. Learn to accept total responsibility for yourself. If you don't manage yourself, then you are letting others have control of your life. In this video you'll discover 90 powerful tips and strategies to better manage yourself for success.

Watch it here:

https://www.bizmove.com/toolkit/self-management.htm

H. Start-Up Costs Worksheet (Excel) – with this tool your start-up costing sheet can be prepared well before you start your business and give you an idea of how much it will cost to start your business.

Get it from here:

https://www.bizmove.com/toolkit/costing.xlsx

I. The Entrepreneur Quiz - A tool to help you assess your entrepreneurship skills. Discover to what extent you have what it takes to succeed as entrepreneur and business owner.

Access it here:

https://www.bizmove.com/toolkit/quiz.ht m

* * *

Thank You for Reading My Book!

And I'm going to ask for a favor...

If you like this book... and if you'd be willing to spare just two or three minutes...would you be willing to share your review of the book on Amazon?

If you would, it would mean the absolute world to me!

Please leave me a supportive review by going to my Amazon book listing and tell me what you think in a review. This helps me get the book into as many hands as possible, helping others to start a successful business!

I really appreciate all your support.

- Meir Liraz

www.ingramcontent.com/pod-product-compliance
Lightning Source LLC
Chambersburg PA
CBHW071217220526
45468CB00002B/648